Best of

British

Eccentricities of an island nation

Compiled by Marion Paull

CICO BOOKS
LONDON NEW YORK

Published in 2011 by CICO Books
An imprint of
Ryland Peters & Small Ltd
20–21 Jockey's Fields   519 Broadway, 5th Floor
London WC1R 4BW   New York, NY 10012

www.cicobooks.com

1 3 5 7 9 10 8 6 4 2

Compilation © Marion Paull 2011
Design © CICO Books 2011

Design by Jacqui Caulton

A CIP catalog record for this book is available from
the Library of Congress and the British Library.

ISBN-13: 978-1-907563-92-8

Printed in China

For digital editions visit
www.cicobooks.com/apps.php

Contents

Introduction

Ask a hundred people to define the essence of Britishness and you'll get a hundred different answers. Is it the quirky sense of humour, the obsession with class or our renowned sense of fair play? Is it always cheering for the underdog? Is it the predilection for queuing, grumbling and talking about the weather, or is it the reticence that hides an unexpected generosity of spirit?

Ask what is the 'Best of British', though, and some names and places, customs and events come up time and again in a characteristically eclectic mix – William Shakespeare, Winston Churchill and Monty Python; Stonehenge, morris dancing and jellied eels; Big Ben, trooping the colour and the Edinburgh Festival. And now David Beckham has been elevated to the status of National Treasure.

This compilaton is loosely divided into sections in an attempt to introduce a modicum of order into all this randomness. It aims just to reflect what is the Best of British and is in no way comprehensive. Not everyone will agree with the selection, of course, which is part of the fun. If these lists and quotations encourage genteel discussions over a cup of Earl Grey and a slice of Victoria sponge, so much the better; or perhaps they will spark more animated debates in the pub, whether that be a low-beamed country pub with roses round the door, or a Dickensian city pub with dark wood and mullioned windows.

On a traditional day out by the seaside, while indulging in that great British treat fish and chips, or while strolling down the pier licking an ice-cream cone, jokes may abound about taking on the Three Peaks Challenge or swimming the channel. You may be surprised to discover that one of you really is going to cycle to Brighton or jump out of a plane at 3,000 feet. To anyone thinking of giving in to such charitable instincts, here's hoping you are filled with that other British characteristic of sheer cussed determination, not to say bloodymindedness – and the best of British luck!

Marion Paull

Food & Drink

"There is no love sincerer than the love of food."

GEORGE BERNARD SHAW (1856–1950)

"*Only dull people are brilliant at breakfast.*"

OSCAR WILDE (1854–1900)

Jamie Oliver

Delia Smith

Mrs Beeton

Full English breakfast

Roast beef and Yorkshire pudding

Bangers and mash

Chicken tikka masala

Left: Fish and chips van c.1935

9

> *"I never thought I'd see the day when I'd be getting f*****g excited over a cup of tea."*

OZZY OSBOURNE

> *"Our trouble is that we drink too much tea. I see in this the slow revenge of the Orient, which has diverted the Yellow River down our throats."*

J.B. PRIESTLEY (1894–1984)

Haggis *Cream tea*

Port and stilton

Real ale

Cider

Scotch whisky

Right: Traditional afternoon tea

10

Pop culture &
the Arts

Music

"The English may not like music, but they
absolutely love the noise it makes."

SIR THOMAS BEECHAM (1879–1961)

*"We were playing a little club in Richmond and
there they were – The Fab Four. The four-
headed monster. They never went anywhere alone."*

**MICK JAGGER, ON INDUCTING THE BEATLES INTO THE
ROCK AND ROLL HALL OF FAME**

Pink Floyd   The Rolling Stones
Sex Pistols

Left: The Beatles appearing on *Top of the Pops*, June 1966

"You have no idea what a poor opinion I have of myself and how little I deserve it."

W.S. GILBERT (1836–1911)

"To me singing is a joy. Choral singing is a delight. Welsh choral singing is more than a delight."

RONNIE BARKER

Elton John

Vera Lynn

Male voice choirs

Brass bands

Last night of the Proms

Vaughan Williams

Gilbert & Sullivan

Elgar

Right: Queen in 1984

"An original idea. That can't be too hard. The library must be full of them."

STEPHEN FRY

"You know, it is a terrible thing to appear on television, because people think that you actually know what you're talking about."

DAVID ATTENBOROUGH

The Goons

Blackadder

Eastenders

Coronation Street

The Archers

Test Match Special

'I'm Sorry I haven't a Clue'

Left: Morecambe and Wise

"I can never do better than Fawlty Towers whatever I do."

JOHN CLEESE

"I don't know what people mean by 'integrity'. I've always found it easier to tell the truth because that way you don't have to remember what you've said. So, for purely practical reasons it is the best thing."

JOHN PEEL (INTERVIEW IN 'THIRD WAY' MAGAZINE)

Monty Python   Blue Peter
X Factor
Strictly Come Dancing
Alan Sugar and The Apprentice
John Peel's Home Truths
Desert Island Discs

Right: Fawlty Towers, 1979

"That's the way to do it."

MR PUNCH

"I find his films about as funny as getting an arrow through the neck and discovering there's a gas bill tied to it."

BLACKADDER (PLAYED BY ROWAN ATKINSON) ON CHARLIE CHAPLIN

Music halls Noel Coward

The Mousetrap

British musicals: *Mary Poppins, Blood Brothers, Wicked, We Will Rock You, Phantom of the Opera*

Left: Punch and Judy

"My formula for living is quite simple. I get up in the morning and I go to bed at night. In between I occupy myself as best I can."

CARY GRANT (1904–1986)

"I have no interest in Shakespeare and all that British nonsense ... I just wanted to get famous. All the rest is hogwash."

SIR ANTHONY HOPKINS

The dames: Edith Evans, Judi Dench, Maggie Smith, Helen Mirren

The knights: Laurence Olivier, Michael Redgrave, John Gielgud, Michael Caine

Old Vic

Carry On films

Pantomime

Right: Barbara Windsor and Sid James in *Carry On Henry*, 1970

Writers, books & artists

"I never travel without my diary. One should always have something sensational to read in the train."

OSCAR WILDE (1854–1900)

"'Curiouser and curiouser,' cried Alice (she was so much surprised, that for the moment she quite forgot how to speak good English).

LEWIS CARROLL (1832–1898) 'ALICE IN WONDERLAND'

Chaucer's Canterbury Tales

Charles Dickens William Shakespeare

Beatrix Potter Lord Byron Jane Austen

Bram Stoker's Dracula

Left: Illustration by John Tenniel, from the 1st edition of *Alice's Adventures in Wonderland*

"And God said, 'Let there be light' and there was light, but the Electricity Board said he would have to wait until Thursday to be connected."

THE BIBLE ACCORDING TO SPIKE MILLIGAN

"We do not write as we want, but as we can."

W. SOMERSET MAUGHAM (1874–1965)

Alan Bennett Agatha Christie

The Wind in the Willows Kenneth Grahame

Winnie the Pooh A.A. Milne

The Lord of the Rings J.R.R. Tolkien

The Chronicles of Narnia C.S. Lewis

George Orwell Ian Fleming's James Bond

Harry Potter and J.K. Rowling

Right: 'Elementary, my dear Watson'

TAKE ME TO YOUR DEALER

"*I have generally found that persons who had studied painting least were the best judges of it.*"

WILLIAM HOGARTH (1697–1764)

Above: Signs Of The Times – work by the graffiti artist Banksy

> *"You're not meant to understand – They're bloody works of art."*

SONIA LAWSON RA

> *"The annual farce of the Turner Prize is now as inevitable in November as is the pantomime at Christmas."*

BRIAN SEWELL

John Constable

George Stubbs

Joseph Mallord William Turner

Tate Britain/Modern

Antony Gormley

Royal Academy

Baltic Flour Mills

David Hockney

29

British Institutions

"History will be kind to me for I intend to write it."

WINSTON CHURCHILL (1874–1965)

"The English know how to make the best of things. Their so-called muddling through is simply skill at dealing with the inevitable."

WINSTON CHURCHILL

Bulldogs *The class system*

BBC the shipping forecast, the World Service, Radio 4 Union Jack

Doctor Who The RSPCA

Fortnum & Mason

Right: Winston Churchill, 1945

> *"Never in the field of human conflict was so much owed by so many to so few."*

WINSTON CHURCHILL ON THE BATTLE OF BRITAIN

> *"Rules are for the obedience of fools and the guidance of wise men."*

DOUGLAS BADER (1910–1982)

Battle of Britain

The Home Guard

'Dad's Army'

the ARP (Air Raid Protection)

Land girls

'Foyle's War'

Right: Spitfire IIa (foreground) and Hawker Hurricane IIc
Above: Lancaster bomber

32

"Well, we were an unbelievably repressed society. Here was this neat little man, conjuring up these quite bawdy images, and people bought them in the millions."

MICHAEL WINNER ON DONALD MCGILL
(INTERVIEW BY JASPER REES FOR
THEARTSDESK.COM)

National Trust

Donald McGill saucy postcards

Harrod's sale

British Museum

Marks & Spencer   The NHS

King James Bible

Dr Johnson's Dictionary

Left: Yeoman Warder, also known as a Beefeater, by Tower Bridge

Lifestyle

"People in England are so bloody nosy."

ELTON JOHN

"The fascination of shooting as a sport depends almost wholly on whether you are at the right or wrong end of the gun."

P.G. WODEHOUSE (1881–1975)

Portobello Road

Cockney rhyming slang **Red telephone box**

Picnics **Gardens and sheds**

Country pubs *Thatched cottages*

Roses around the door

Carnaby Street and King's Road

Huntin', shootin', fishin' and wellies and Barbours

Left: A Boxing Day hunt

37

Customs & festivals

"You should try everything once except incest
and morris dancing."

VARIOUSLY ATTRIBUTED

*"The city is famous for the arts (it was once
known as 'the Athens of the North')."*

FROM 'HANDSOME EDINBURGH'

Bonfire night

Notting Hill Carnival

Edinburgh Festival

Village fete

Maypole dancing

Changing of the Guard

Right: Morris dancers

"Fashion is very important. It is life-enhancing and,
like everything that gives pleasure, it is worth doing well."

VIVIENNE WESTWOOD

"Fashion should be a game."

MARY QUANT

Harris Tweed
Fair Isle jumpers
Trench coats

Punk

*Bowler hat, pinstriped
suit and furled umbrella*

Left: Vivienne Westwood

41

> *"Is there anything worn under the kilt? No, it's all in perfect working order."*

SPIKE MILLIGAN (1918–2002)

> *"It's not what you'd call a figure, is it?"*

TWIGGY

Sixties' style

Mini skirts

Alexander McQueen

Twiggy

Topshop

Tartan

Kate Moss

Right: Twiggy with the winner of a lookalike competition

Trains & boats & planes & cars & buses

"Not all those who wander are lost."

J.R.R. TOLKIEN (1892–1973)

"You're only supposed to blow the bloody doors off!"

CHARLIE CROKER (PLAYED BY MICHAEL CAINE IN 'THE ITALIAN JOB')

"With the casino and the beds, our passengers will have at least two ways to get lucky on one of our flights."

RICHARD BRANSON

Rolls-Royce *Aston Martin*

Bubble cars *Morris Minor*

Black cabs

Left: Mini Cooper

"This iconic new part of our transport system is not only beautiful, but also has a green heart beating beneath its stylish, swooshing exterior ..."

BORIS JOHNSON ON UNVEILING THE NEWLY DESIGNED
VERSION OF THE ROUTEMASTER BUS

"The only way to be sure of catching a train is to miss the one before it."

G.K. CHESTERTON (1874–1936)

Flying Scotsman

Tube trains

Hovercraft

Queen Mary & QEII

Royal Yacht Britannia

Right: Old Routemaster bus

46

Sport & Games

"'The game,' he said, 'is never lost til won.'"

GEORGE CRABBE (1754–1832) GRETNA GREEN

"I love scoring goals for England and playing for England. That's one of the reasons I didn't retire — I love playing for my country."

DAVID BECKHAM

1966 World Cup winners   *The Derby*

FA Cup   *Ascot*

Boxing   Gymkhana and Pony Club

London marathon and Great North Run

Left: David Beckham, 2006

49

> *"I love tennis with a passion. I challenged Boris Becker to a match once and he said he was up for it but he never called back. I bet I could make him run around."*

BORIS JOHNSON

Village cricket

2003 Rugby World Cup

MCC The Ashes 2005

Boat race

Henley

Rugby club

conkers

Pub quiz

Right: Sunny day at Wimbledon

Great scientists & inventors

"It is not the strongest of the species that survives, nor the most intelligent that survives. It is the one that is the most adaptable to change."

CHARLES DARWIN (1809–1882)

"I thought 'The Martians have arrived!', but then I realised that I was looking at pollen slightly out of focus."

PATRICK MOORE (IN THE 'OBSERVER', MARCH 2003)

"I have noticed even people who claim everything is predestined, and that we can do nothing to change it, look before they cross the road."

STEPHEN HAWKING

Left: Charles Darwin, 1902

> *"The key to success is to risk thinking unconventional thoughts. Convention is the enemy of progress. As long as you've got slightly more perception than the average wrapped loaf, you could invent something."*

TREVOR BAYLIS, INVENTOR OF THE CLOCKWORK RADIO

Isaac Newton Tim Berners-Lee

George and Robert Stephenson

Alan Turing John Logie Baird

Sir Barnes Wallis

Stephen Hawking

Sir James Dyson

Sir Clive Sinclair

Alexander Graham Bell

Right: Isambard Kingdom Brunel, c.1850

Landmarks

"Was it a temple for sun worship, a healing centre, a burial site or perhaps a huge calendar? Surrounded by mystery, Stonehenge never fails to impress."

ENGLISH HERITAGE

Hadrian's Wall

Tower of London

York Minster

Tyne bridges *St Paul's*

the millennium wheel

Whitby Abbey

Left: Stonehenge, Amesbury, Wiltshire

> *"There'll be bluebirds over the white cliffs of Dover,*
> *Tomorrow, just you wait and see"*

'THE WHITE CLIFFS OF DOVER' – NAT BURTON,
MADE FAMOUS BY DAME VERA LYNN

Giant's Causeway

Loch Ness

Blackpool

Glastonbury Tor

Cheddar Gorge

Southend pier

Lakes and fells of Cumbria

Right: White cliffs of Dover. Inset: Vera Lynn, 1965
Below: Brighton beach

The Royals

"You are a member of the British royal family. We are never tired,
and we all love hospitals."

QUEEN MARY

Queen Victoria

Duchess of Kent *The Queen Mother*

George VI *Princess Diana*

Left: William and Kate's official engagement photo
Below: The Queen with her family on the balcony at Buckingham Palace

"*You must not miss Whitehall. At one end you'll find a statue of one of our kings who was beheaded; at the other, the monument to the man who did it. This is just an example of our attempts to be fair to everybody.*"

SIR EDWARD APPLETON (1892–1965)

"*I know I have the body of a weak and feeble woman, but I have the heart and stomach of a King, and of a King of England too.*"

ELIZABETH I'S SPEECH TO THE TROOPS AT TILBURY, 1588

Boudicca   King Arthur

Henry V

Alfred the Great   *Elizabeth I*

Mary, Queen of Scots   George III

Right: Portrait of Henry VIII by Holbein the Younger